RISING STARS

**ASSESSMENT**



# Science Progress Tests

## Year 5

**Steve Bunce**

**Series Advisors: Cornwall Learning**

RISING STARS

CORNWALL LEARNING

Rising Stars UK Ltd, 7 Hatchers Mews, Bermondsey Street, London SE1 3GS

www.risingstars-uk.com

Published 2014
Reprinted 2014 (three times), 2015



All facts are correct at time of going to press.

Author: Dr. Steve Bunce
Educational consultant: Ed Walsh, Cornwall Learning
Accessibility reviewer: Vivien Kilburn
Editorial: Denise Moulton and Lynette Woodward
Typist: Rosalyn Dale
Design: Ray Rich and Clive Sutherland
Illustrations: Oxford Designers and Illustrators
Cover design: Burville-Riley Partnership

Rising Stars is grateful to the following people and schools who contributed to the development of these materials.
Plumcroft Primary School, London; Rainford Brook Lodge Primary School, Merseyside; St Nicholas CE Primary School, Chislehurst; St Margaret's CE Primary School, Heywood, Rochdale; Tennyson Road Primary School, Luton



British Library Cataloguing in Publication Data.
A CIP record for this book is available from the British Library.
ISBN: 978 1 84680 964 4

FSC www.fsc.org MIX Paper from responsible sources FSC® C011748

Printed by Ashford Colour Press

# Contents

# Introduction

### Why use Rising Stars Assessment Progress Tests?

The *Rising Stars Assessment Science Progress Tests* have been developed to support teachers assess the progress their pupils are making against the 2014 National Curriculum Programme of Study for science. The tests are designed to support effective classroom assessment across Years 1 to 6 and are easy to use and mark.

The tests are organised around the topics in the Programme of Study and have been:

- written by primary science assessment specialists
- reviewed by primary science curriculum and assessment experts.

### How do the tests track progress?

The results data from the tests can be used to track progress. They show whether pupils are making the expected progress for their year, more than expected progress or less than expected progress. This data can then be used alongside other evidence to enable effective planning of future teaching and learning, for reporting to parents and as evidence for Ofsted inspections. If teachers are using the CD-ROM version of the tests, the results data can be keyed into the Progress Tracker (see page 7 for more information) which automatically shows the progress of individual pupils against the Programme of Study and the results for all pupils by question and test. Data can also be exported into the school's management information system (MIS).

### About the Science Progress Tests

The tests are written to match the content requirements of the Programme of Study for the 2014 National Curriculum. The content areas are:

| Content | Year 1 | Year 2 | Year 3 | Year 4 | Year 5 | Year 6 |
|---|---|---|---|---|---|---|
| Living things (and their habitats) | | ✓ | | ✓ | ✓ | ✓ |
| Plants | ✓ | ✓ | ✓ | | | |
| Animals, including humans | ✓ | ✓ | ✓ | ✓ | ✓ | ✓ |
| Evolution and inheritance | | | | | | ✓ |
| Materials (uses, properties and changes) | ✓ | ✓ | | | ✓ | |
| Rocks | | | ✓ | | | |
| States of matter | | | | ✓ | | |
| Light | | | ✓ | | | ✓ |
| Sound | | | | ✓ | | |
| Seasonal changes/Earth and space | ✓ | | | | ✓ | |
| Forces (and magnets) | | | ✓ | | ✓ | |
| Electricity | | | | ✓ | | ✓ |

In line with the Programme of Study, the skills of working scientifically are assessed through all the content areas rather than separately. For each content area there are four tests:

- Test 1(diagnostic) – note that for Years 1 and 2 this is a checklist rather than a test to make it more accessible and informative for pupils whose written language skills are likely to be less developed

- Test 2(mid-topic)
- Test 3(end of topic)
- Test 4(end of year) The marks for each test are as follows:

| Test | Number of marks | | | | | |
|---|---|---|---|---|---|---|
| | Year 1 | Year 2 | Year 3 | Year 4 | Year 5 | Year 6 |
| Test/checklist 1 (diagnostic) | N/A | N/A | 10 | 10 | 10 | 10 |
| Test 2 (mid-topic) | 10 | 10 | 10 | 10 | 10 | 10 |
| Test 3 (end of topic) | 10 | 10 | 10 | 10 | 10 | 10 |
| Test 4 (end of year) | 10 | 10 | 10 | 10 | 10 | 10 |

### *Test demand*

The first test for each topic is designed to help teachers assess the prior learning of individual pupils and the class before teaching begins. These tests/checklists are more open-ended than tests 2–4 to elicit as much information as possible to help teachers to refine their plans for teaching the topic.

Test 2 is designed to be used during a topic, test 3 at the end of a topic and test 4 at the end of the year. Test 4 could optionally be used as an alternative or additional test at the end of a topic. Tests 2–4 follow the same approach. In each test:

- 5 marks are allocated to knowledge and understanding
- 5 marks are allocated to application
- 4 marks additionally assess working scientifically.

Tests 2–4 also contain a mix of objective questions, and questions requiring written answers.

### *Tracking progress*

The marks pupils score in the tests can be used to track how they are progressing against the expected outcomes for their year group in relation to the National Curriculum Programme of Study. The marks for tests 2–4 for each topic have been split into three progress zones:

- less than expected progress
- expected progress
- more than expected progress.

The zones for each year group are as follows:

| | | Zone mark range | | |
|---|---|---|---|---|
| | Test | Less than expected progress | Expected progress | More than expected progress |
| Year 1 | 2–4 | 0–5 | 6–8 | 9–10 |
| Year 2 | 2–4 | 0–5 | 6–8 | 9–10 |
| Year 3 | 2–4 | 0–5 | 6–8 | 9–10 |
| Year 4 | 2–4 | 0–5 | 6–8 | 9–10 |
| Year 5 | 2–4 | 0–5 | 6–8 | 9–10 |
| Year 6 | 2–4 | 0–5 | 6–8 | 9–10 |

The table gives the mark ranges for the progress zones for each test which you can use to see how well each pupil is doing in each test. If pupils are making the expected progress for their year they will be consistently scoring marks in the middle zone of marks in the tests. The higher the mark in the zone, the more secure you can be that they are making expected progress.

### Determining prior learning

The first test for each topic is provided to help teachers find out about prior learning.

For Years 1 and 2 these tests are in the form of diagnostic checklists to enable an oral investigation of prior learning as it is recognised that pupils have limited reading and writing vocabularies, particularly in Year 1. Each checklist comprises a set of questions to ask pupils and supporting visual prompts. There is also a Pupil responses form that can be used to record whether some, most or all pupils are able to answer each question.

For Years 3–6 there is a diagnostic test for each topic. These tests can be administered as described below and the marks analysed to identify the prior learning of individual pupils and the class as a whole.

## How to use the Science Progress Tests

### *Preparation and timings*

**1** Make enough copies of the test(s) for each pupil to have their own copy.
**2** Hand out the papers and ensure pupils are seated appropriately so that they can't see each other's papers.
**3** Pupils will need pens or pencils, rulers and erasers. Encourage pupils to cross out answers rather than rub them out.
**4** There are no time limits for the tests but normal practice is to allow a minute per mark for written tests. Help with reading may be given using the same rules as when providing a reader with the DfE KS2 tests.

### *Supporting pupils during the tests*

Before the test explain to the pupils that the test is an opportunity to show what they know, understand and can do. They should try to answer all the questions but should not worry if there are some they can't do.

Many pupils will be able to work independently in the tests, with minimal support from the teacher or a teaching assistant. However, pupils should be encouraged to 'have a go' at a question, or to move on to a fresh question if they appear to be stuck, to ensure that no pupil becomes distressed.

It is important that pupils receive appropriate support, but are not unfairly advantaged or disadvantaged. Throughout the tests, therefore, the teacher may read, explain or sign to a pupil any parts of the test that include instructions, for example by demonstrating how to circle an answer.

With younger age groups you may also consider using the version of the test on the CD-ROM and projecting it onto a whiteboard to support a whole class or group to take the tests. You may choose to refer to the words on the whiteboard and read them aloud so that pupils can follow them on the screen and on their own test paper and then write their answers on their papers individually.

### *Marking the tests*

Use the detailed mark scheme and your professional judgement to award marks. **Do not award half marks.**

It is useful to use peer marking of test questions from time to time. Pupils should exchange test sheets and mark them as you read out the question and answer. You will need to check that pupils are marking accurately. This approach also provides an opportunity to recap on any questions that pupils found difficult to answer.

### *Feeding back to pupils*

Once the test has been marked, use a five-minute feedback session with the pupils to help them review their answers. Wherever possible pupils should be encouraged to make their own corrections as in this way they will become more aware of their own strengths and weaknesses. Agree with each pupil what they did well in the test and what the targets are for them to improve. A template Pupil progress sheet is provided on page 8 for this purpose.

## Using the Progress Tracker

The table on page 5 gives the mark ranges for the progress zones for each test which you can use to see how well each pupil is doing in each test. If pupils are making the expected progress for their year they will be consistently scoring marks in the middle zone of marks in the tests. The higher the mark in the zone, the more secure you can be that they are making expected progress.

The CD-ROM* version of *Science Progress Tests* includes an interactive Progress Tracker, which allows you to enter the marks for each question for each test by pupil. This then automatically shows you which zone the pupil is in and also the zone distribution for the class so that you can track the progress of individual pupils and the whole class.

The Progress Tracker also enables you to review the marks for each question so that you can identify areas where some or all pupils may need further support and areas where some or all pupils are ready to be stretched further.

If required, data from the tests can be exported into the school's management information system (MIS) so that it can be used alongside other data in whole school monitoring including the monitoring of specific groups of pupils, such as Pupil Premium.

Full details about the Progress Tracker are provided on the CD-ROM.

* If you have the book version only of *Science Progress Tests*, the Progress Tracker can be downloaded from bit.ly/progtracker

# Pupil progress sheet

Name: ______________________ Class: ____________ Date: __________

Topic name: ______________________ Test number: ____ My mark: _____

What I did well in the test:

______________________________________________

______________________________________________

______________________________________________

What I need to do to improve:

1. ______________________________________________

2. ______________________________________________

3. ______________________________________________

- - - - - - - - - - - - - - - - - - - - - - - - - - - - -


# Pupil progress sheet

Name: ______________________ Class: ____________ Date: __________

Topic name: ______________________ Test number: ____ My mark: _____

What I did well in the test:

______________________________________________

______________________________________________

______________________________________________

What I need to do to improve:

1. ______________________________________________

2. ______________________________________________

3. ______________________________________________

# Year 5
# **Living things and their habitats** Test 1 (diagnostic)

Name: ______________________ Class: ____________ Date: __________

**1. a)** Put the numbers in the correct place to show the order of the human life cycle.

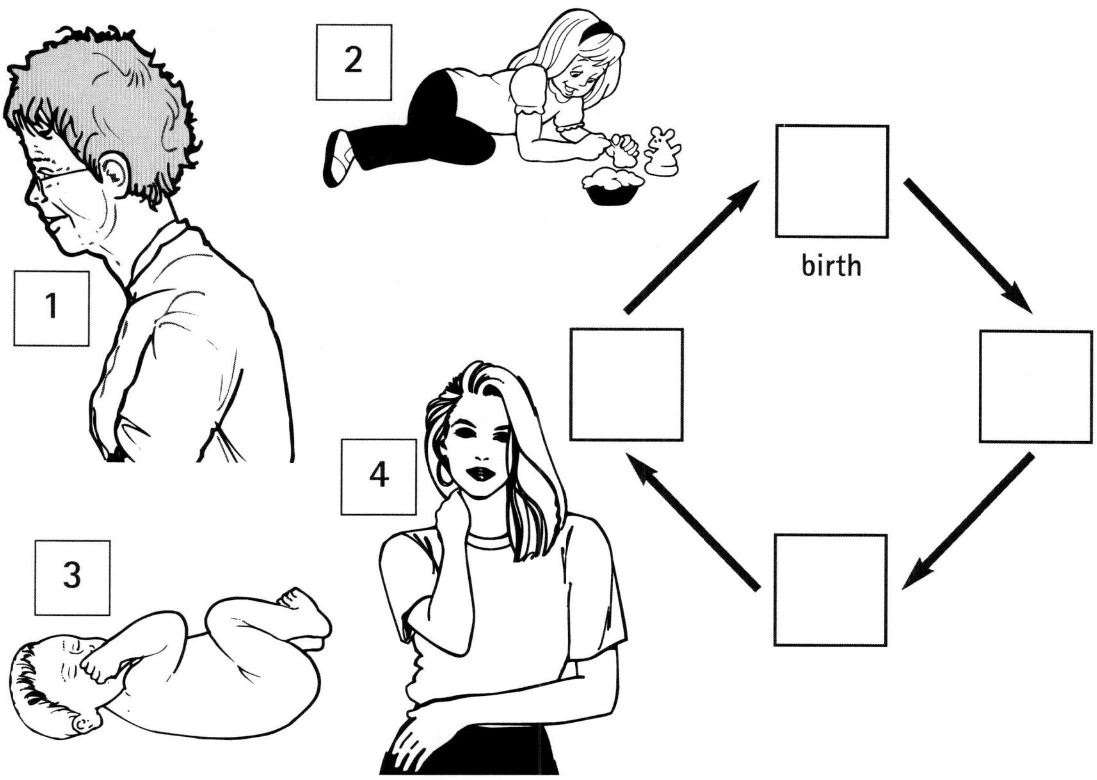


KU
1 mark

**b)** A frog begins as an egg, then it becomes a tadpole, then a tadpole with legs and finally an adult frog. How could you find out the time it takes to change from a tadpole into a tadpole with legs?

..............................................................................................................

A/WS
1 mark

**c)** In which units would you measure the time between the stages of a frog's life cycle? Choose from seconds, hours or days.

..........................................

A/WS
1 mark

**d)** Compare the human and the frog life cycle. Give **one** difference.

..............................................................................................................

..............................................................................................................

A
1 mark

Total for this page

**2.** Put the steps of the plant life cycle in order. Put the letters in the correct place.

**A pollination**

**B germination**

**C seed dispersal**

**D flowering**

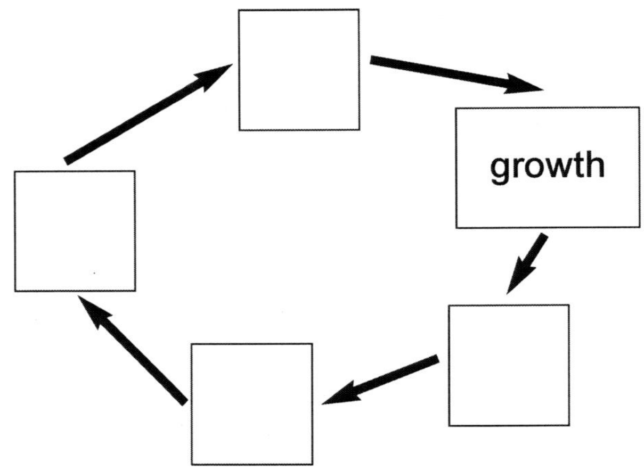


KU
2 marks

**3.** **a)** Two parts of this flower have been labelled. Label the other two.

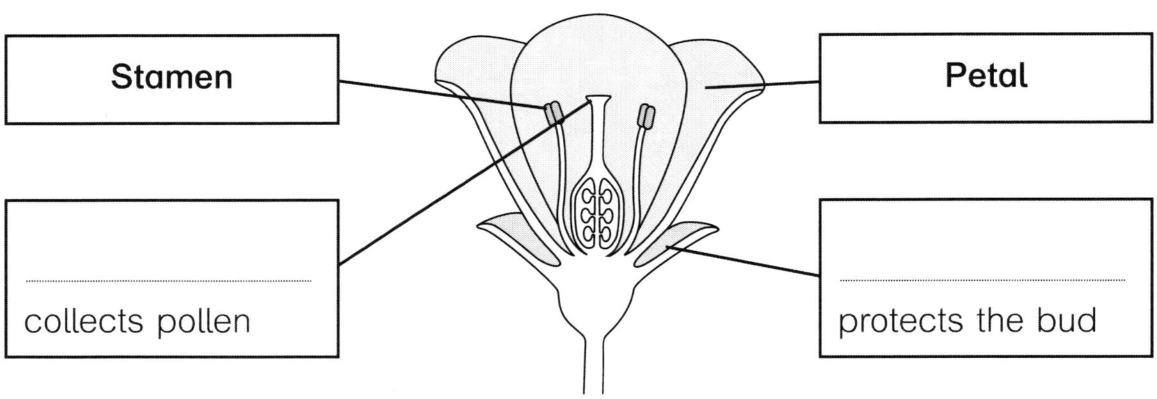


KU
1 mark

**b)** Why do some flowers have petals?

..........

KU
1 mark

**4.** Describe an experiment to see if yellow flowers or white flowers attract more bees.

..........

..........

..........

..........

A/WS
2 marks

/10
**Total for this test**

Year 5

# Living things and their habitats Test 2 (mid-topic)

Name: ______________________ Class: ____________ Date: __________

**1.** A blackbird and a caterpillar both hatch from eggs. Compare the blackbird and the caterpillar life cycles. Give **one** difference.

..............................................................................................................

KU

1 mark

**2.** **a)** Suggest how you could investigate the life cycle of caterpillars.

..............................................................................................................

..............................................................................................................

A/WS

1 mark

**b)** How might you be able to tell if a caterpillar is alive?

..............................................................................................................

A

1 mark

**3.** Name **two** things a seed needs to start growing.

..............................................................................................................

KU

2 marks

**4.** Complete the labels in the boxes and join them to the correct parts of the flower.

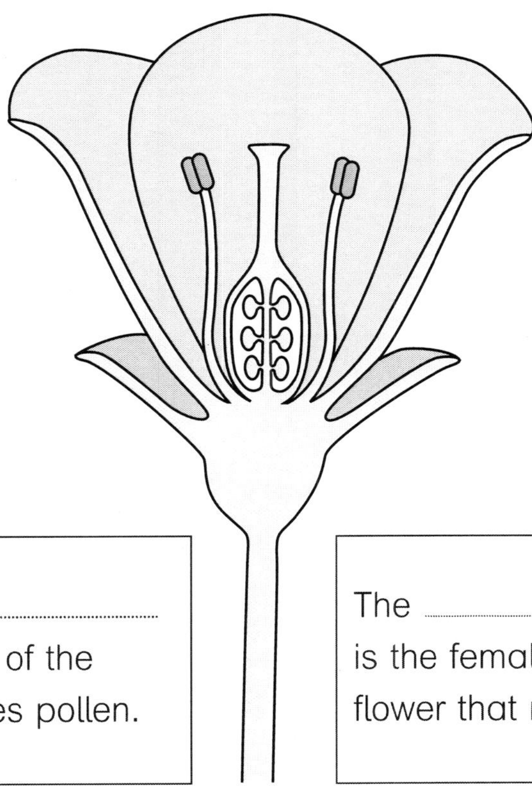

The .................................. is the male part of the flower that makes pollen.

The .................................. is the female part of the flower that receives pollen.

KU

2 marks

Total for this page

**5.** Monika collects data on flowers in her garden.
The chart shows what she finds.

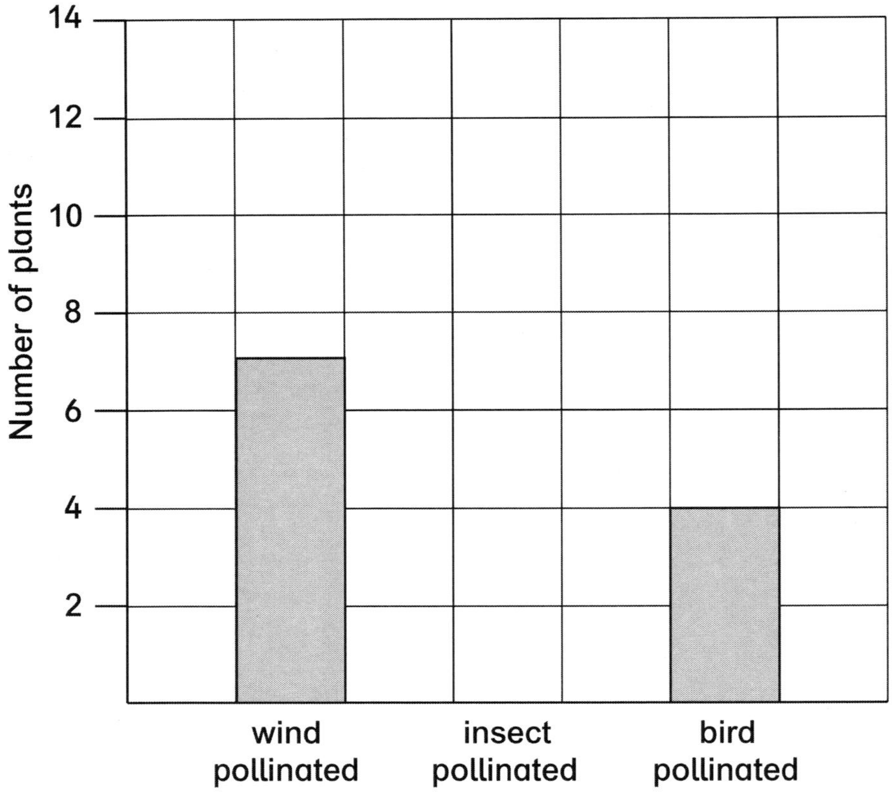


**a)** How many plants are wind pollinated? Circle the correct answer.

A/WS 1 mark

6 7 8

**b)** There were 11 insect pollinated plants. Complete the chart to show this.

A/WS 1 mark

**c)** How many plants did Monika investigate altogether? ..........................

A/WS 1 mark

/10 **Total for this test**

# Year 5
# **Living things and their habitats** Test 3 (end of topic)

Name: ______________________ Class: ______________ Date: __________

**1.** The graph shows the number of red wolves in the wild.

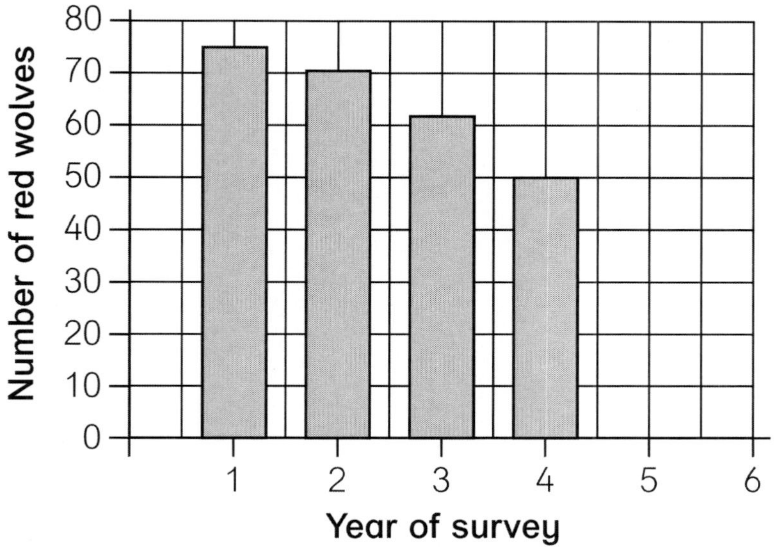


A/WS

1 mark

**a)** What was the population in year 3? ..............................

A/WS

1 mark

**b)** Write the year when the population was 50. ..............................

A/WS

1 mark

**c)** Estimate the bar graph for years 5 and 6 to show what will happen to the wolf population if it continues to fall in the same way.

**2.** **a)** Give **two** different ways that plants can be pollinated.

i) ..............................

ii) ..............................

KU

2 marks

**b)** Why might a plant **not** be pollinated?

..............................

A

1 mark

**c)** Choose the correct word to complete the sentence below:

sepal stigma petal stem

In pollination, pollen is transferred onto the plant's .............................. .

KU

1 mark

Total for this page

**3.** **a)** How are these seeds likely to be dispersed?
Join each seed to the correct answer.

A

B

| using the wind | sticking to animals | bursting open | shaking seed pods |
|---|---|---|---|

KU
2 marks

**b)** How could you find out if all of the flowers on a plant become seeds?

.......................................................................................................

.......................................................................................................

A/WS
1 mark

/10
**Total for this test**

Year 5

# **Living things and their habitats** Test 4 (end of year)

Name: ______________________ Class: ____________ Date:

**1.** Put these life cycles in order from longest to shortest.

frog human fly

.............................................................................................................

**longest**

KU

1 mark

**2.** **a)** Why does a tadpole lose its gills and form lungs when it becomes a frog?

Tick the correct answer.

Frogs need lungs to breathe on land. ☐

Lungs are lighter than gills. ☐

Frogs need lungs to eat flies. ☐

KU

1 mark

**b)** Why is a frog considered to be an amphibian?

.............................................................................................................

.............................................................................................................

KU

1 mark

**3.** a) Name the process that changes an animals appearance.

______________________________

KU

2 marks

b) Give an example of an animal that goes through this and explain its life cycle.

______________________________

______________________________

______________________________

Total for this page

4) Define a mammal:

1 mark

___________________________________________

5) a) What does the word 'endangered' mean?

1 mark

___________________________________________

b) Give ② examples of ways in which humans are helping animals complete their life cycles.

2 mark

___________________________________________

___________________________________________

___________________________________________

___________________________________________

6) Why are bees endangered? How could you help bees in your garden?

1 Mark

Total

10 marks

# Year 5

# Living things and their habitats Test 4 (end of year)

Name: ______________________ Class: ____________ Date:

**1.** Put these life cycles in order from longest to shortest.

frog    human    fly

..............................................................................................

**longest**

KU
1 mark

**2.** **a)** Why does a tadpole lose its gills and form lungs when it becomes a frog?

Tick the correct answer.

Frogs need lungs to breathe on land. ☐

Lungs are lighter than gills. ☐

Frogs need lungs to eat flies. ☐

KU
1 mark

**b)** Why is a frog considered to be an amphibian?

..............................................................................................

..............................................................................................

KU
1 mark

**3.** Coconut palms grow on beaches. Coconuts are dispersed by floating away on the water. Give **two** other ways in which seeds are dispersed.

i) ..............................................................................................

ii) ..............................................................................................

KU
2 marks

Total for this page

 

**4.** Sam wants to find out more about the germination of different seeds.

**a)** What question could she investigate?

..............................................................................................................

..............................................................................................................

A/WS

1 mark

**b)** What variable could she change?

..............................................................................................................

A/WS

1 mark

**c)** What variable could she measure or count in her test?

..............................................................................................................

A/WS

1 mark

**d)** How could she measure this variable?

..............................................................................................................

..............................................................................................................

A/WS

1 mark

**e)** Explain why some of the seeds in her experiment might not germinate.

..............................................................................................................

..............................................................................................................

A

1 mark

/10

**Total for this test**

Year 5

# **Animals, including humans** Test 1 (diagnostic)

Name: ____________________ Class: ____________ Date: __________

**1.** **a)** A foetus is a baby that is growing inside its mother's womb.
Circle the correct answer.

**true** **false**

KU
1 mark

**b)** How long does a human baby normally stay inside the mother?
Tick the correct answer.

3 months ☐

5 months ☐

9 months ☐

KU
1 mark

**2.** Suggest why a camel has a longer gestation time than humans.

........................................................................

........................................................................

A
1 mark

**3.** Write **two** key words you could use to research the gestation time of other mammals on the Internet.

.................................... ....................................

A/WS
2 marks

Total for this page

**4.** David is ten years old.
How will his bones change over the next two years?

..........................................................................................

..........................................................................................

KU
1 mark

**5.** Name **two** changes to a boy's body at puberty.

**i)** ..........................................................................................

**ii)** ..........................................................................................

KU
2 marks

**6.** How could you show that an adult has stopped growing?

..........................................................................................

..........................................................................................

A/WS
2 marks

/10
**Total for this test**

Year 5

# **Animals, including humans** Test 2 (mid-topic)

Name: ______________________ Class: ______________ Date: __________

**1.** What does a foetus need when inside its mother?
Tick **all** the correct answers.

milk ☐ protection ☐

air ☐ food ☐

water ☐ toys ☐

KU ☐ 2 marks

**2.** Suggest a way to show that a baby is growing.

........................................................................

........................................................................

........................................................................

........................................................................

A/WS ☐ 2 marks

**3.** Pupils in Class 5 want to compare the size of feet of adults and Year 5 pupils.

**a)** What could the pupils use to measure the feet?

........................................................................

KU/WS ☐ 1 mark

**b)** Suggest a good method they could use to display their results.

........................................................................

A/WS ☐ 1 mark

☐ Total for this page

**4.** Why do children go through puberty?

KU

2 marks

**5.** Most animals lay eggs. It is only mammals that have the young growing inside them.

Give **two** similarities between these two forms of reproduction.

A

2 marks

/10

**Total for this test**

Year 5

# **Animals, including humans** Test 3 (end of topic)

Name: ____________________ Class: ____________ Date: __________

**1.** A giraffe can carry its foetus for up to 16 months. Is that more or less than a human? Circle the correct answer.

**more** **less**

KU

☐

1 mark

**2.** Why do you think newborn babies need more sleep than a two-year-old?

.............................................................................................................................

.............................................................................................................................

A

☐

2 marks

**3.** When babies are born they cannot walk. Can other mammals walk as soon as they are born?

Write **two** key words you could use to search the Internet to find out.

.................................................... ....................................................

A/WS

☐

1 mark

**4.** Puberty only happens to girls. Circle the correct answer.

**true** **false**

KU

☐

1 mark

☐

Total for this page

**5.** Ravinder thinks all the boys are taller than the girls in his class.

**a)** What would he use to measure their heights?

KU/WS

1 mark

**b)** How could Ravinder check that his measurements are accurate?

A/WS

1 mark

**c)** How could he find out the speed at which children grow?

A/WS

1 mark

**6.** Which names apply to the stages in our life cycle that happen from a child to an adult? Circle the correct answers.

**adulthood** **puberty** **teenager**

**birth** **death** **reproduction**

KU

2 marks

/10

**Total for this test**

Year 5

# Animals, including humans Test 3 (end of topic)

Name: ____________ Class: ____________ Date: ____________

1. A giraffe can carry its foetus for up to 16 months. Is that more or less than a human? Circle the correct answer.

more less

KU 1 mark

2. (A) What name is given to a flower which has both the male and female parts in the same flower? ____________

A 2 marks

(B) What is the name of the process where a bee passes pollen from one flower to another? ____________

3. There is a type of stick insect which appears to only have females. How can this be?

A/WS 1 mark

4. Puberty only happens to girls. Circle the correct answer.

true false

KU 1 mark

Total for this page

Year 5

# **Animals, including humans** Test 4 (end of year)

Name: ______________________ Class: ____________ Date: __________

**1.** Order the timeline of human life. Put these words in the correct places. The first one has been done for you.

**old age** **adulthood** **baby** **adolescence** **childhood**

1. foetus
2. ........................................
3. ........................................
4. ........................................
5. ........................................
6. ........................................

KU

☐

3 marks

**2.** Plan a test to show how a baby's weight changes in the first three months of its life.

........................................................................................................

........................................................................................................

........................................................................................................

A/WS

☐

2 marks

☐

Total for this page

**3.** **a)** Suggest a likely value for the missing measurement and write it in the table.

| **Bone** | **Length age 6** | **Length age 10** |
|---|---|---|
| lower arm | | 18 cm |
| leg | 50 cm | 75 cm |

A/WS
1 mark

**b)** Give a reason for your answer.

........................................................................................................................

........................................................................................................................

A/WS
1 mark

**4.** Give **one** change in girls during puberty.

........................................................................................................................

KU
1 mark

**5.** Give **one** change in boys during puberty.

........................................................................................................................

KU
1 mark

**6.** An old person is still growing taller. Circle the correct answer.

**true** **false**

A
1 mark

/10
**Total for this test**

# Year 5

## **Properties and changes of materials** Test 1 (diagnostic)

Name: ______________________ Class: ____________ Date: __________

**1.** Place these materials into two groups. Label the groups.

**steel** **iron** **plastic** **glass**

A/WS

1 mark

**2.** **a)** Carys mixes some powders with water. Tick the solutions.

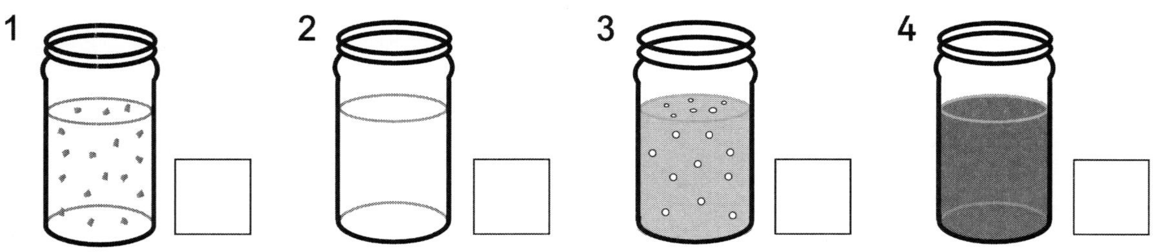

KU

1 mark

**b)** Carys mixes salt, sand and water.

How can she separate the sand from the mixture?

KU/WS

1 mark

Total for this page

**3.** The sea is salty. Why is rainwater not salty?

A

2 marks

**4.** Jess has three spoons. One spoon is made of metal, one is made of wood and one is made of plastic. How could she find out which spoon would stay coolest when stirring hot water?

A/WS

2 marks

**5.** Complete the following table.

| | **What happens when heated strongly?** |
|---|---|
| butter | |
| water | |
| egg | |

KU

3 marks

/10

**Total for this test**

Year 5

# **Properties and changes of materials** Test 2 (mid-topic)

Name: ______________________ Class: ____________ Date: __________

**1.** **a)** Name one solid that dissolves.

..................................................................................................

A [ ] 1 mark

**b)** Solids that cannot dissolve are called ...................................................... .

KU [ ] 1 mark

**2.** Amy puts three different powders into three beakers of water.
Match the beaker or beakers to the sentences in the table.
One has been done for you.

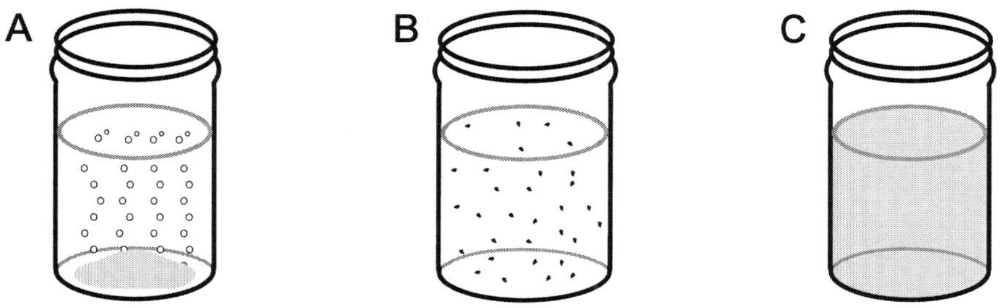


| | |
|---|---|
| It has made a solution. | |
| It has bubbles in it. | A |
| It can be separated by filtering. | |
| It cannot be separated by filtering. | |
| It can only be separated by evaporation. | |
| It is making a gas. | |
| You can still see the powder. | |
| It is a chemical change. | |

KU [ ] 4 marks

[ ] Total for this page

 

**3.** Dan wants a new ruler. He can buy a ruler made of wood, or one made of metal, or one made of plastic.

How can he test which ruler would not get scratched?

........................................................................................................

........................................................................................................

........................................................................................................

........................................................................................................

A/WS ☐ 2 marks

**4.** When chocolate is heated, it melts.

How could you show that this is a reversible change?

........................................................................................................

........................................................................................................

A/WS ☐ 1 mark

**5.** When acid is added to bicarbonate of soda, it is an irreversible change.

Why do you think this change is irreversible?

........................................................................................................

........................................................................................................

A/WS ☐ 1 mark

☐ /10

**Total for this test**

# Year 5
## **Properties and changes of materials** Test 3 (end of topic)

Name: ______________________ Class: ____________ Date: ________

**1.** Mrs Callow is conducting a test to see how different materials burn in a candle flame.

Give **two** ways she could make the test safe.

i) ........................................................................

ii) ........................................................................

A/WS ☐ 2 marks

**2.** Name **two** new materials that are made when paper burns.

.................................... and ....................................

KU ☐ 2 marks

**3.** **a)** Tick those materials that will burn in a candle flame.

**cotton wool** ☐

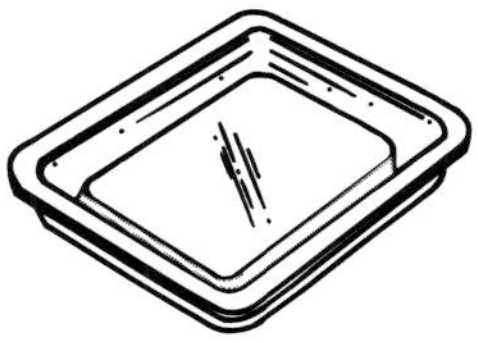

**foil dish** ☐

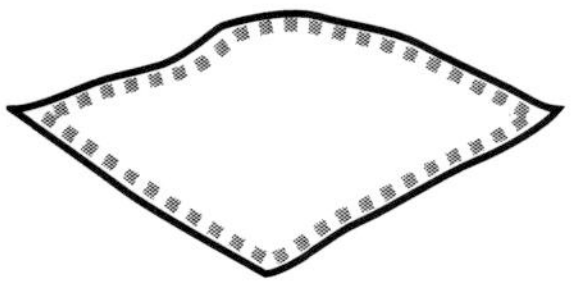

**cloth** ☐

**2p coin** ☐

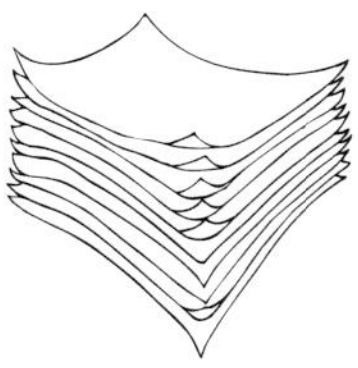

**paper** ☐

KU ☐ 2 marks

**b)** Name **one** other material that will burn in a candle flame.

........................................................................

KU ☐ 1 mark

**c)** What material could a candle holder be made of?

........................................................................

A ☐ 1 mark

☐ Total for this page

**4.** Ella wants to investigate what things affect the time it takes salt to dissolve in a beaker of water.

**a)** What question could she test?

A/WS

1 mark

**b)** What variable does she need to change in her test?

A/WS

1 mark

/10

**Total for this test**

# Year 5

## **Properties and changes of materials** Test 4 (end of year)

Name: ______________________ Class: ____________ Date: __________

**1.** **a)** Circle the **two** solids that will dissolve in water.

**salt** **sand** **sugar** **flour**

KU
2 marks

**b)** When a solid dissolves in a liquid, it makes a ______________________ .

KU
1 mark

**c)** Where does the dissolved solid go?

______________________________________________

KU
1 mark

**2.** Ajay mixes a powder with water. It doesn't dissolve.

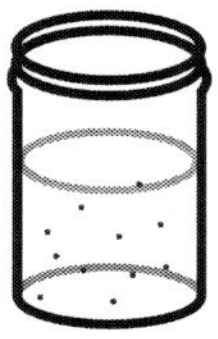

**a)** What can he use to separate this mixture?

______________________________________________

A/WS
1 mark

**b)** How does that work?

______________________________________________

______________________________________________

A/WS
1 mark

**3.** Salt is dissolved in water. Describe how to separate the salt from the water.

______________________________________________

______________________________________________

______________________________________________

A/WS
2 marks

Total for this page

 

**4.** Becky puts some fizzy orange and some ice cubes in a glass.
She observes drops of liquid appearing on the outside of the glass.

**a)** Name the process that causes liquid to appear on the outside of the glass.

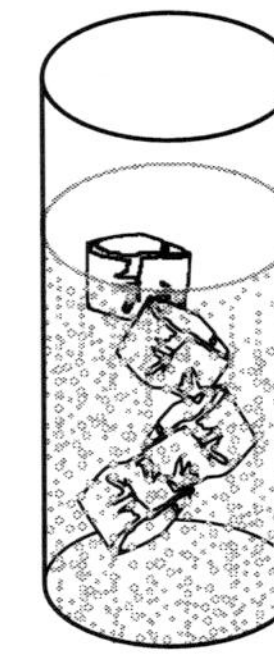

KU

1 mark

**b)** What colour will this liquid be?

A

1 mark

/10

**Total for this test**

Year 5

# **Earth and space** Test 1 (diagnostic)

Name: ______________________ Class: ____________ Date: ________

**1.** **a)** Label the Earth, the Sun and the Moon.

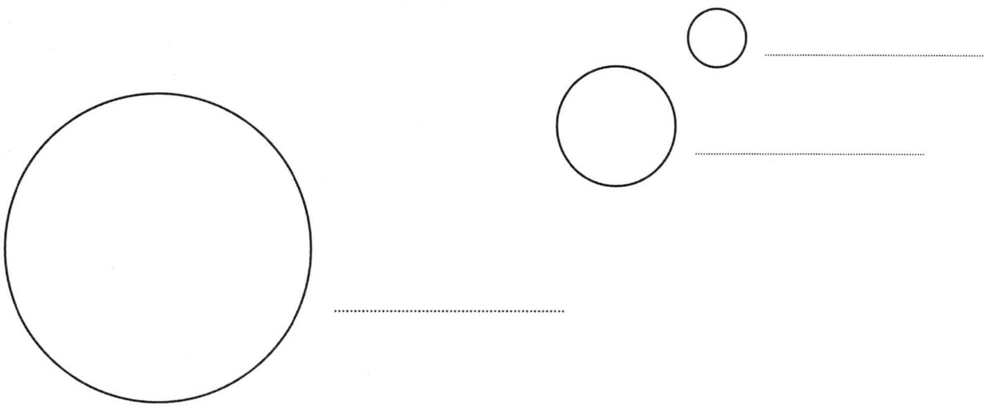

KU

2 marks

**b)** Shade the Earth to show night and day.

KU

1 mark

**c)** Cross out **one** key word you would **not** use to search the Internet to find the shape of the Earth.

**Earth** **shape** **space**

A

1 mark

**2.** Tick the **two** sentences that are correct.

The Earth orbits the Sun. ☐

The Earth orbits the Moon. ☐

The Moon orbits the Sun. ☐

The Sun orbits the Earth. ☐

The Sun orbits the Moon. ☐

The Moon orbits the Earth. ☐

KU

2 marks

Total for this page

**3.** How could you find out if the Sun rises in the east?

..........

..........

A/WS

2 marks

**4.** How could you prove that days are longest in the summer?

..........

..........

A/WS

2 marks

/10

**Total for this test**

Year 5

# **Earth and space** Test 2 (mid-topic)

Name: ______________________ Class: ____________ Date: __________

**1.** **a)** Which of these planets orbit the same sun as the Earth?
Tick the correct answers.

Mars ☐

Neptune ☐

KU ☐ 2 marks

**b)** Which of these planets has the higher surface temperature?
Tick the correct answer.

Mars ☐

Neptune ☐

KU ☐ 1 mark

**2.** **a)** How long does it take for the Moon to orbit the Earth?

..............................................................................................

KU ☐ 1 mark

**b)** How long does it take for the Earth to orbit the Sun?
Circle the correct answer.

**1 day** **1 month** **1 year**

KU ☐ 1 mark

☐ Total for this page

**3.** Mrs Butcher's class keeps a record of sunrise and sunset times every Monday for eight weeks. The pupils put their results in a graph.

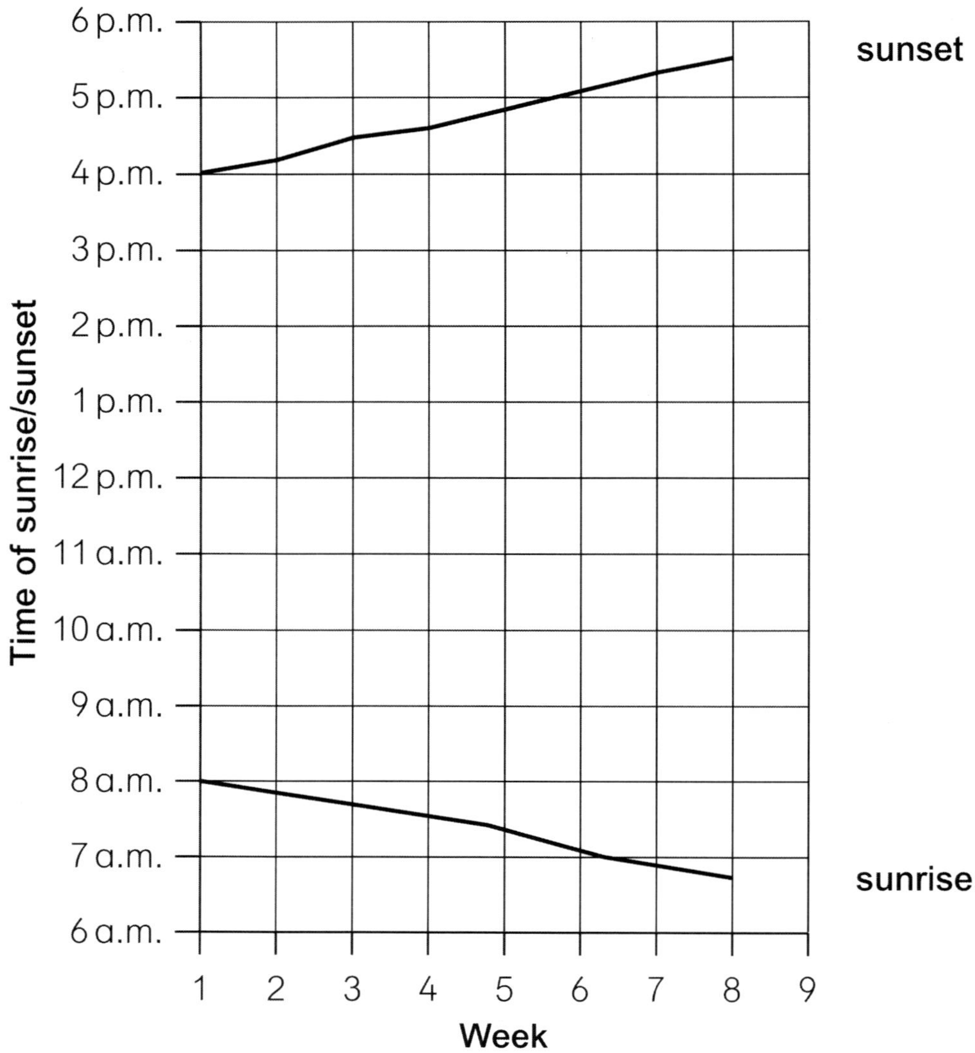


**a)** Complete the sentence below using these words:

**later** **earlier** **longer**

Over the eight weeks, sunrise gets .................... and sunset gets .................... , so the daylight time gets .................... .

A/WS

1 mark

A/WS

2 marks

**b)** Continue both lines on the graph for week 9.

A/WS

1 mark

**c)** Sunrise in week 2 was at .................... .

A

1 mark

**d)** Were the pupils doing this experiment in spring or autumn?

....................................................................................................

/10

**Total for this test**

Year 5

# **Earth and space** Test 3 (end of topic)

Name: ______________________ Class: ____________ Date: __________

**1.** Amy is finding out about the Moon.

**a)** What does the Moon orbit?

.......................................................................................................

KU

1 mark

**b)** How long does this orbit take?

.......................................................................................................

KU

1 mark

**2.** Daniel is finding out about the Earth.

**a)** How long does it take for the Earth to spin once on its axis?

.......................................................................................................

KU

1 mark

**b)** Draw a diagram showing how the the Sun, Earth and the Moon are arranged, and showing what orbits what.

KU

2 marks

Total for this page

**3.** Class 5 found out, from the Internet, how many hours of daylight there were each day over the year. The pupils made the following graph.

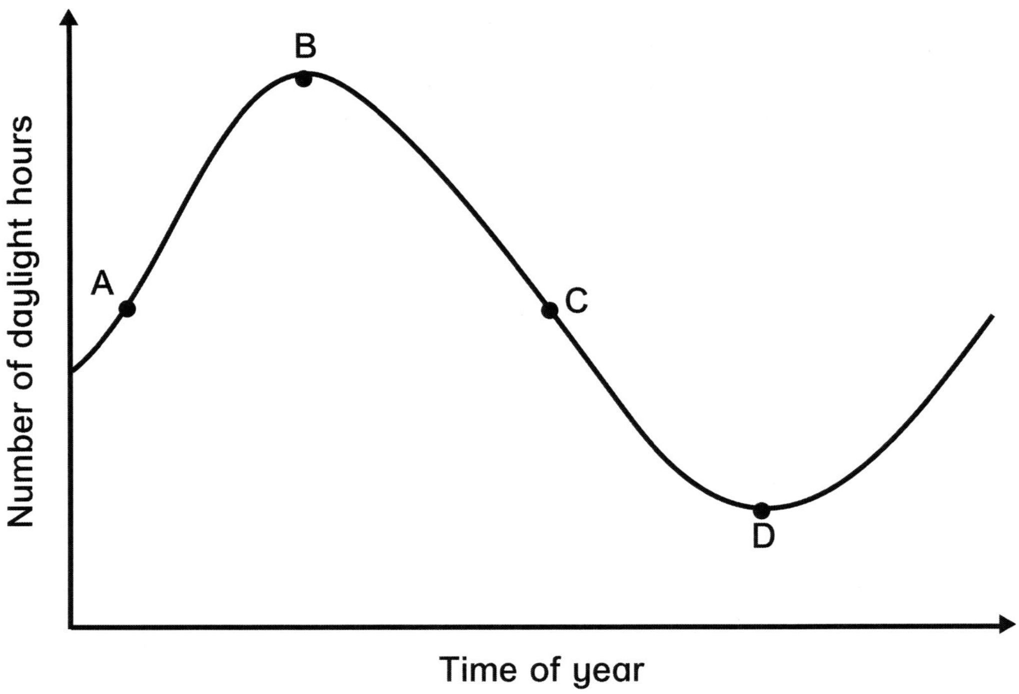


**a)** Which point on the graph is in June? ..........

A/WS
1 mark

**b)** Which point on the graph is in December? ..........

A/WS
1 mark

**c)** Place two crosses on the graph to show when the hours of daylight are the same in spring and autumn.

A
1 mark

**d)** What conclusion can you draw from this pattern of results?

..........

..........

A/WS
2 marks

/10
**Total for this test**

Year 5

# **Earth and space** Test 4 (end of year)

Name: ______________________ Class: ____________ Date: __________

**1.** How could you record the phases of the Moon?

........................................................................................................

........................................................................................................

KU/WS ☐ 2 marks

**2.** How long does it take for the Moon to orbit the Earth once?

Tick the correct answer.

1 month ☐

6 months ☐

12 months ☐

KU ☐ 1 mark

**3.** Rachel lives in England. She is investigating the Sun.

Write north, south, east or west in each space in the table.

| **Time of day** | **Where will Rachel see the Sun?** |
|---|---|
| early morning | |
| midday | |
| evening | |

A ☐ 3 marks

☐ Total for this page

**4.** The drawing shows the Sun at 2 p.m. You are looking south.

A/WS

1 mark

**a)** Draw the shadow at noon.

A/WS

1 mark

**b)** Draw where the Sun was at 10 a.m.

**c)** Why does the Sun appear to move?

..................................................

..................................................

..................................................

KU

2 marks

/10

**Total for this test**

Year 5

# **Forces** Test 2 (mid-topic)

Name: ______________________ Class: ____________ Date: __________

**1.** **a)** What units are used to measure a force?

______________________

KU

1 mark

**b)** Which force pulls a parachute towards the Earth?

Tick the correct answer.

friction ☐

gravity ☐

mass ☐

KU

1 mark

**c)** What is the effect of air resistance on a parachute?

Tick the correct answer.

It slows down the parachute's fall. ☐

It speeds up the parachute's fall. ☐

KU

1 mark

**d)** These parachutes all have the same load.

Tick the parachute that will fall fastest.

A

☐

B

☐

C

☐

A

1 mark

**e)** How could you make this parachute fall more slowly?

______________________________________________

A/WS

1 mark

**f)** What could you use to measure the falling time?

______________________

A/WS

1 mark

Total for this page

**2.** **a)** What is the name of the force that slows down objects moving in water?

KU

1 mark

b) Explain how forces in water affect an object.

A/WS

2 marks

c) Tell me the forces acting on this boat:

KU

1 mark

/10

**Total for this test**

Year 5

# **Forces** Test 1 (diagnostic)

Name: ______________________ Class: ______________ Date: __________

**1.** If a ball is dropped, it falls because of the force of gravity between it and the Earth. Circle the correct answer.

**true** **false**

KU
☐
1 mark

**2.** Gravity is only found on the Earth. Circle the correct answer.

**true** **false**

KU
☐
1 mark

**3.** A box slides over a surface.

**a)** When two surfaces rub together, what is the name of the force that opposes the movement?

..............................................................................................................

KU
☐
1 mark

**b)** Explain what would happen to this force if the surfaces were made smoother.

..............................................................................................................

..............................................................................................................

A
☐
1 mark

**c)** How will this affect the force needed to move the box?

..............................................................................................................

..............................................................................................................

A
☐
1 mark

☐
Total for this page

**4.** **a)** What is this called? ..........

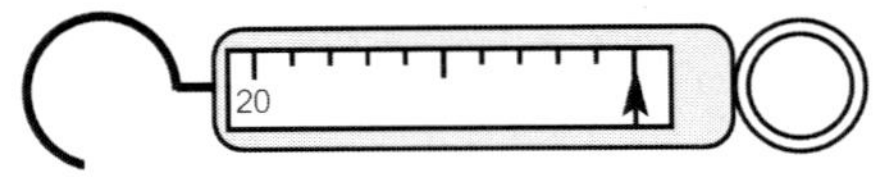


KU/WS 1 mark

**b)** What units measure force? ..........

KU/WS 1 mark

**c)** What size force is pulling box A? ..........

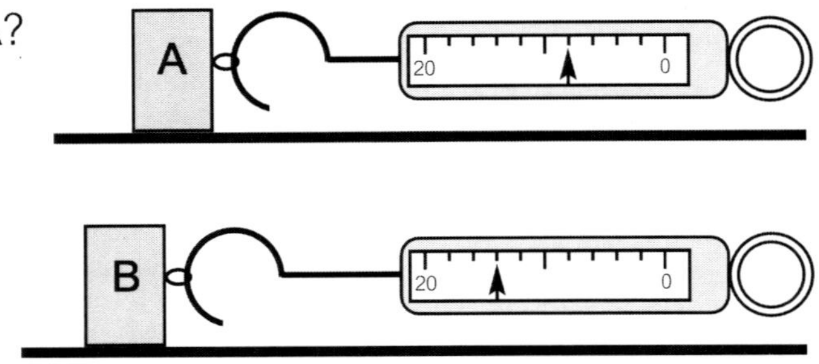


A/WS 1 mark

**d)** Which box is harder to move? ..........

A/WS 1 mark

**5.**

A lever placed under a block can lift it.

A large movement of the lever moves the block with .......... effort.

Choose the correct word to complete the sentence above: **less** **more**

A 1 mark

/10 **Total for this test**

Year 5
# **Forces** Test 2 (mid-topic)

Name: ______________________ Class: ____________ Date: __________

**1. a)** What units are used to measure a force? | KU 1 mark

______________________

**b)** Which force pulls a parachute towards the Earth?
Tick the correct answer.

friction ☐

gravity ☐

mass ☐

KU 1 mark

**c)** What is the effect of air resistance on a parachute?
Tick the correct answer.

It slows down the parachute's fall. ☐

It speeds up the parachute's fall. ☐

KU 1 mark

**d)** These parachutes all have the same load.
Tick the parachute that will fall fastest.

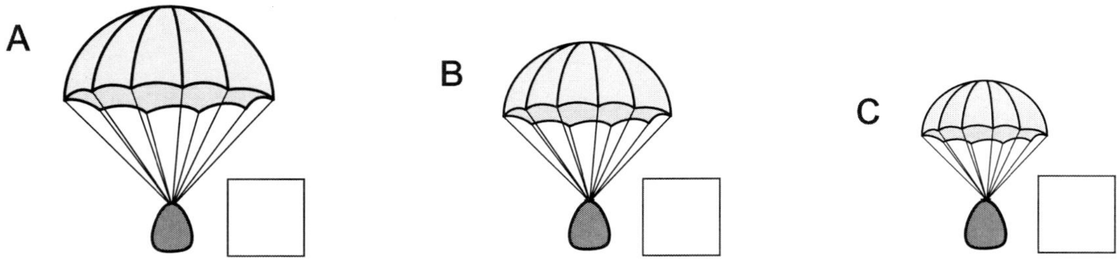


A 1 mark

**e)** How could you make this parachute fall more slowly?

______________________

A/WS 1 mark

**f)** What could you use to measure the falling time?

______________________

A/WS 1 mark

Total for this page

**2.** **a)** What is the name of the force that slows down objects moving in water?

KU

1 mark

**b)** Alex is making boats.

How could he find out which shape moves fastest in the water?

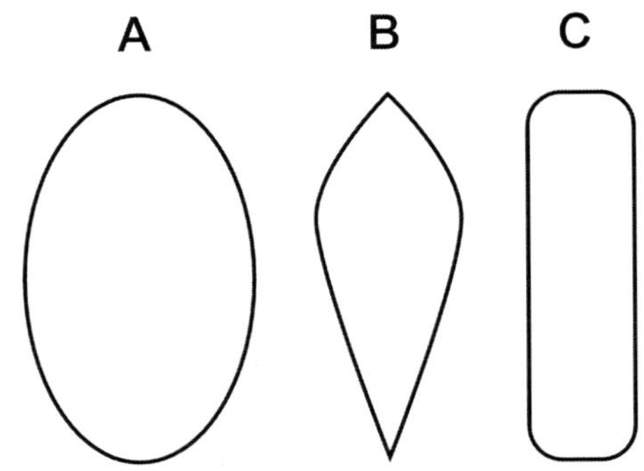


A/WS

2 marks

**3.** Why does a bike have gears?

KU

1 mark

/10

**Total for this test**

# Year 5
# **Forces** Test 3 (end of topic)

Name: ______________________ Class: ____________ Date: __________

**1.** Circle **all** the forces.

**weight** **height** **gravity** **friction**

KU

1 mark

**2.** a) Draw and label arrows to show the direction of air resistance in this diagram.

KU

1 mark

b) Draw and label arrows to show the direction of friction in this diagram.

KU

1 mark

Total for this page

**3.** **a)** Raksha pulls a block across different surfaces to test the effect of

.................................................. .

KU 1 mark

**b)** What could Raksha use to measure the force?

..................................................

KU/WS 1 mark

**c)** Raksha makes a table of her results.

| **Surface** | **Force to pull block over surface, in N** |
|---|---|
| rubber sheet | 8 |
| carpet | 16 |
| woven hessian cloth | 11 |
| smooth plastic | 4 |

Which surface causes most friction?

..................................................

A/WS 1 mark

**d)** How does the table show this?

..................................................

A/WS 1 mark

**e)** What should Raksha conclude from her test?

..................................................

..................................................

A/WS 1 mark

**4.** Scissors are a type of lever. Explain how scissors work.

..................................................

..................................................

..................................................

A 2 marks

/10 **Total for this test**

Year 5

# **Forces** Test 4 (end of year)

Name: ______________________ Class: ____________ Date: __________

**1.** Class 5 pupils are investigating five different sized parachutes made from the same material.

**a)** Which force pulls the parachutes towards the Earth?

..............................................................

KU
1 mark

**b)** Which force slows the parachutes down?

..............................................................

KU
1 mark

**c)** The pupils drop each parachute from the **same** height with the **same** mass tied on. Explain why.

..............................................................

A/WS
1 mark

**d)** The pupils measure the time for the parachute to fall.
What units would they use?

..............................................................

KU/WS
1 mark

Total for this page

**e)** Class 5 pupils draw a graph of their results. Label the two axes.
Choose from time, mass, distance or width of parachute.

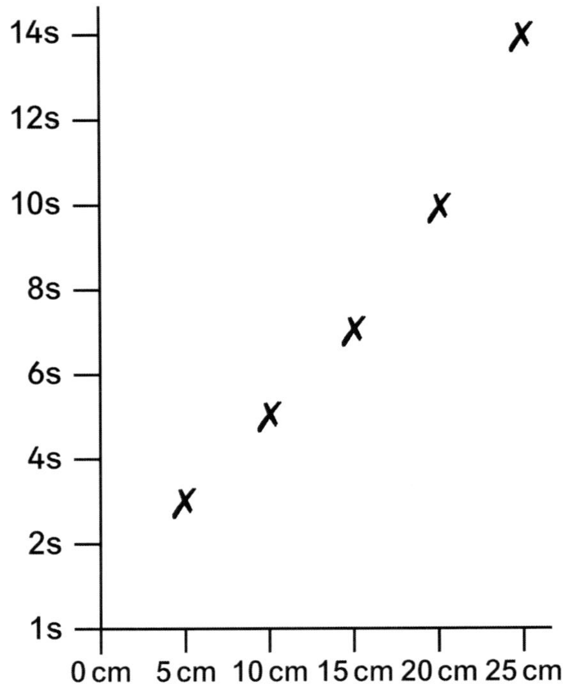


A/WS
1 mark

**f)** What is your conclusion from the graph?

........................................................................................................................

........................................................................................................................

A/WS
1 mark

**g)** Explain why using a parachute makes it possible to jump out of an aircraft and land safely.

........................................................................................................................

........................................................................................................................

........................................................................................................................

........................................................................................................................

A
2 marks

**2.** A pulley on a ship allows a rope to be pulled to lift a weight.
Compare the size of the force the person applies with the size of the force acting on the weight.

........................................................................................................................

........................................................................................................................

KU
2 marks

/10
**Total for this test**

# Answers and mark schemes

## Year 5 Living things and their habitats

| Test 1 (diagnostic) | Area | Mark | Extra information |
|---|---|---|---|
| **1a.** Clockwise: 3 (birth), 2, 4, 1 | KU | 1 | |
| **1b.** Observe the frog every day and record the changes by drawings, photographs or written descriptions. Record the time between hatching and growing back legs. | A/WS | 1 | |
| **1c.** Days | A/WS | 1 | |
| **1d.** Human cycle is longer.<br>Frog begins in water then grows legs later, changing from underwater living to amphibious living. | A | 1 | Accept any reasonable difference |
| **2.** Clockwise from growth: D flowering, A pollination, C seed dispersal, B germination | KU | 2 | |
| **3a.** Stigma to collect pollen, sepal to protect the bud | KU | 1 | Both correct for 1 mark |
| **3b.** To attract insects | KU | 1 | |
| **4.** Description of a test to count the number of bees visiting the yellow flowers in comparison with the white flowers. | A/WS | 2 | 1 mark for description of test<br>1 mark for comparison |

| Test 2 (mid-topic) | Area | Mark | Extra information |
|---|---|---|---|
| **1.** Caterpillar becomes a pupae and then a butterfly. Blackbird becomes a young bird, before an adult bird. | KU | 1 | Accept any reasonable difference |
| **2a.** Description of an investigation: observing over time, interviewing an expert, reading a book, watching a film. | A/WS | 1 | Accept any reasonable investigation method |
| **2b.** Description of looking for the caterpillar moving, eating, growing or responding to changes around it. | A | 1 | Accept any reasonable answer |
| **3.** Any **two** from: warmth, water, air | KU | 2 | |
| **4.** Labels correctly completed and joined for stamen and stigma. | KU | 2 | 1 mark for each label correctly completed and joined |
| **5a.** 7 | A/WS | 1 | |
| **5b.** Column drawn to 11. | A/WS | 1 | Should be roughly the same width as the other bars |
| **5c.** 22 | A/WS | 1 | If the answer to question 5a was incorrect and the error is carried forward to question 5c, accept the answer |

## Living things and their habitats (continued)

| Test 3 (end of topic) | Area | Mark | Extra information |
|---|---|---|---|
| **1a.** 62 | A/WS | 1 | Accept 61, 62 or 63 |
| **1b.** Fourth year/year 4 | A/WS | 1 | |
| **1c.** Both bars continue falling. | A/WS | 1 | |
| **2a.** Any **two** from: insects, wind, animals, birds | KU | 2 | |
| **2b.** Any **one** from: might die, might not be visited by insects, might not be in a good place to catch wind | A | 1 | Accept any reasonable explanation |
| **2c.** Stigma | KU | 1 | |
| **3a.** A: sticking to animals<br>B: using the wind | KU | 1<br>1 | |
| **3b.** Description of an enquiry to count the number of flowers on a plant and then to count how many become seeds. | A/WS | 1 | |

| Test 4 (end of year) | Area | Mark | Extra information |
|---|---|---|---|
| **1.** Human, frog, fly | KU | 1 | 1 mark for all three correct |
| **2a.** Frogs need lungs to breathe on land. | KU | 1 | |
| **2b.** Because during their life frogs change from living in the water to living on the land. | KU | 1 | |
| **3.** Any **two** from: wind, explosion, sticking to animals, shaking, animal food, drop and roll | KU | 2 | 1 mark for each correct answer |
| **4a.** Any **one** from:<br>Do all seeds germinate at the same time (or temperature)?<br>How long does it take for different types of seeds to germinate?<br>How many seeds that are planted germinate?<br>Do seeds germinate as quickly in a dark/cool place as in a light/warm place?<br>Do seeds that germinate sooner grow taller? | A/WS | 1 | Accept any reasonable enquiry |
| **4b.** Any **one** from: soil, water, temperature, time or types of seeds | A/WS | 1 | |
| **4c.** Any **one** from: when the seeds germinate, how many seeds germinate | A/WS | 1 | Accept any reasonable answer (depending on the answers to the previous questions) |
| **4d.** Any plausible indication of how the variable indicated in question 4c could be measured, e.g. counting the number of seedlings if germination rates are being investigated. | A/WS | 1 | |
| **4e.** Any **one** from: might have died, might be damaged, too little or too much water, too low or too high a temperature | A | 1 | |

## Animals, including humans

| Test 1 (diagnostic) | Area | Mark | Extra information |
|---|---|---|---|
| **1a.** True | KU | 1 | |
| **1b.** 9 months | KU | 1 | |
| **2.** It's larger than a human, and the larger the animal the longer the gestation period tends to be. | A | 1 | Accept because it's bigger |
| **3.** Any **two** from: gestation, pregnancy, mammals, babies | A/WS | 2 | Accept any two reasonable answers |
| **4.** They will grow longer. | KU | 1 | Accept become stronger |
| **5.** Any **two** from: becomes more muscular, voice deepens, body hair develops, shoulders widen, genitals grow | KU | 2 | 1 mark for each correct |
| **6.** Description of test measuring an adult and then measuring them again after a time period to compare the two measurements. | A/WS | 2 | 1 mark for describing a test<br>1 mark for comparison |

| Test 2 (mid-topic) | Area | Mark | Extra information |
|---|---|---|---|
| **1.** Protection, air, food, water | KU | 2 | 2 marks for all four correct<br>1 mark for two or three correct |
| **2.** Description of a test to measure the baby and measuring it over time. | A/WS | 2 | 1 mark for describing a test to measure the baby<br>1 mark for measuring over time |
| **3a.** Metre stick, tape measure | KU/WS | 1 | Accept ruler |
| **3b.** Any suitable method, e.g. graph, table, tally chart | A/WS | 1 | |
| **4.** To become adults capable of having children. | KU | 2 | 1 mark for indicating that puberty results in adulthood<br>1 mark for referring to child rearing |
| **5.** Any **two** from: protect developing young, provide food, allow for growth | A | 2 | 1 mark for each correct |

## Animals, including humans (continued)

| Test 3 (end of topic) | Area | Mark | Extra information |
|---|---|---|---|
| **1.** More | KU | 1 | |
| **2.** Newborn babies are growing more rapidly and so need more sleep. | A | 2 | 1 mark for reference to growth<br>1 mark for indicating that growth requires sleep |
| **3.** Any **two** from: baby, walk, start, human, mammal, birth | A/WS | 1 | Accept any two reasonable answers for 1 mark |
| **4.** False | KU | 1 | |
| **5a.** Metre stick, tape measure. | KU/WS | 1 | Accept ruler |
| **5b.** Any **one** from: repeat the reading, check with another measuring device, ask someone else to take the reading, average several readings | A/WS | 1 | |
| **5c.** Description of an enquiry measuring the children over a time period. | A/WS | 1 | |
| **6.** Puberty, teenager | KU | 2 | 1 mark for each correct |

| Test 4 (end of year) | Area | Mark | Extra information |
|---|---|---|---|
| **1.** 1 foetus, 2 baby, 3 childhood, 4 adolescence, 5 adulthood, 6 old age | KU | 3 | 3 marks for all five correct<br>2 marks for four correct<br>1 mark for two or three correct |
| **2.** Description of a test to weigh the baby.<br>Plan to weigh the baby over the time period of three months. | A/WS | 2 | 1 mark for planning a test to weigh the baby<br>1 mark for weighing the baby over time |
| **3a.** Between 10 and 14 cm | A/WS | 1 | |
| **3b.** Bones grow as a child grows.<br>Leg is half as long again so arm probably is too. | A/WS | 1 | Accept one reasonable answer |
| **4.** Any **one** from: develop breasts, hips widen, body hair develops, periods begin | KU | 1 | Accept one reasonable answer |
| **5.** Any **one** from: become more muscular, voice deepens, body hair develops, shoulders widen | KU | 1 | Accept one reasonable answer |
| **6.** False | A | 1 | |

## Properties and changes of materials

| Test 1 (diagnostic) | Area | Mark | Extra information |
|---|---|---|---|
| **1.** Materials placed into two groups based on a reasonable label, e.g. hardness, solubility, transparency, conductivity (electrical and thermal), response to magnets, metal/not metal. | A/WS | 1 | Any reasonable grouping and label required for 1 mark |
| **2a.** 2 and 4 | KU | 1 | Both correct for 1 mark |
| **2b.** Use filter paper to remove sand, and then evaporation to remove water. | KU/WS | 1 | Accept the mixture is filtered |
| **3.** When water evaporates the salt is left behind. This water may then form rain clouds. | A | 2 | 1 mark referring to clouds formed as result of evaporation<br>1 mark for indicating salt is left behind<br>Accept rain is condensed water that has evaporated |
| **4.** Description of method and comparison of materials. | A/WS | 2 | 1 mark for describing an enquiry<br>1 mark for comparison |
| **5.** Butter melts.<br>Water evaporates or boils.<br>Egg cooks or there is a chemical change. | KU | 1<br>1<br>1 | <br><br>Accept goes hard |

| Test 2 (mid-topic) | Area | Mark | Extra information |
|---|---|---|---|
| **1a.** E.g. salt or sugar | A | 1 | Accept any reasonable answer |
| **1b.** Insoluble | KU | 1 | |
| **2.** It has made a solution. **C**<br>[It has bubbles in it. A]<br>It can be separated by filtering. **A & B**<br>It cannot be separated by filtering. **C**<br>It can only be separated by evaporation. **C**<br>It is making a gas. **A**<br>You can still see the powder. **A & B**<br>It is a chemical change. **A** | KU | 4 | 4 marks for all seven correct<br>3 marks for five or six correct<br>2 marks for three or four correct<br>1 mark for two correct |
| **3.** Description of a test of the hardness of the material (e.g. by scratching with another object).<br>Description of comparing the materials. | A/WS | 2 | 1 mark for a test of hardness<br>1 mark for comparison of materials |
| **4.** Cool the chocolate and it will go hard again (although possibly in a different shape). | A/WS | 1 | |
| **5.** The original materials cannot be remade from the new material that has been made. | A/WS | 1 | |

# Properties and changes of materials (continued)

| Test 3 (end of topic) | Area | Mark | Extra information |
|---|---|---|---|
| **1.** Any **two** from: use tea light or low candle; use tongs to hold the material; put sand round the candle; put the candle in a dish; use special gloves | A/WS | 2 | 1 mark for each correct |
| **2.** Ash or smoke<br>Carbon dioxide or gas | KU | 1<br>1 | Accept water |
| **3a.** Cotton wool, cloth, paper | KU | 2 | 2 marks for all three correct<br>1 mark for two correct |
| **3b.** Anything else that will burn in a candle flame. | KU | 1 | Accept any reasonable answer |
| **3c.** Any non-flammable material, e.g. steel, brass, copper | A | 1 | |
| **4a.** What effect will the amount of salt/the amount of water/the temperature of water/the amount of stirring/ the size of crystals have on how long it takes the salt to dissolve? | A/WS | 1 | 1 mark for any reasonable question |
| **4b.** Whatever was identified in the question posed in **4a**, e.g. volume of water, temperature of water. | A/WS | 1 | |

| Test 4 (end of year) | Area | Mark | Extra information |
|---|---|---|---|
| **1a.** Salt and sugar | KU | 2 | 1 mark for each correct |
| **1b.** Solution | KU | 1 | |
| **1c.** It goes into the liquid. | KU | 1 | |
| **2a.** Filter paper | A/WS | 1 | |
| **2b.** The filter paper has tiny holes that let the water through but will not let little pieces of solid through. | A/WS | 1 | |
| **3.** Evaporate the liquid and the solid is left behind (the liquid could be collected by condensation on a cold glass nearby). | A/WS | 2 | 1 mark for evaporation<br>1 mark for indicating this will leave the solid behind |
| **4a.** Condensation | KU | 1 | |
| **4b.** Colourless | A | 1 | Accept clear |

## Earth and space

| Test 1 (diagnostic) | Area | Mark | Extra information |
|---|---|---|---|
| **1a.** Sun largest, Earth middle, Moon smallest | KU | 2 | 2 marks for all three correct<br>1 mark for one or two correct |
| **1b.** Side of Earth facing away from Sun is shaded.<br>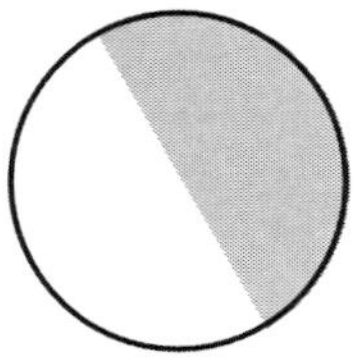 | KU | 1 | |
| **1c.** 'Space' crossed out. | A | 1 | |
| **2.** The Earth orbits the Sun.<br>The Moon orbits the Earth. | KU | 1<br>1 | |
| **3.** Use a compass to find the east.<br>Watch the Sun rise. | A/WS | 1<br>1 | |
| **4.** Measure the length of days in various part of the year.<br>Record and compare. | A/WS | 1<br>1 | |

| Test 2 (mid-topic) | Area | Mark | Extra information |
|---|---|---|---|
| **1a.** Mars, Neptune | KU | 2 | 1 mark for each correct |
| **1b.** Mars | KU | 1 | |
| **2a.** 1 month | KU | 1 | Accept approximately 28–30 days |
| **2b.** 1 year | KU | 1 | |
| **3a.** Earlier, later, longer | A/WS | 1 | All correct for 1 mark |
| **3b.** Sunrise line continues to fall.<br>Sunset line continues to rise. | A/WS | 1<br>1 | |
| **3c.** 7.40–8.00 a.m. | A/WS | 1 | |
| **3d.** Spring | A | 1 | |

## Earth and space (continued)

| Test 3 (end of topic) | Area | Mark | Extra information |
|---|---|---|---|
| **1a.** The Earth | KU | 1 | |
| **1b.** 1 month | KU | 1 | Accept approximately 28–30 days |
| **2a.** 24 hours | KU | 1 | Accept 1 day |
| **2b.** Basic diagram showing the Moon orbiting the Earth and the Earth orbiting the Sun. | KU | 2 | 1 mark for each correct orbit |
| **3a.** B | A/WS | 1 | |
| **3b.** D | A/WS | 1 | |
| **3c.** Two crosses are placed at equal heights on the graph. | A | 1 | Since autumn spans from halfway between points B & C to halfway between C & D, accept an answer anywhere in this section with a corresponding cross at the same height for spring |
| **3d.** The number of daylight hours varies over the year. | A/WS | 2 | Accept a more detailed explanation, if correct, e.g. the tilt or angle of the Earth towards the Sun alters through the year<br>1 mark for a partial response, e.g. sometimes it's lighter |

| Test 4 (end of year) | Area | Mark | Extra information |
|---|---|---|---|
| **1.** Draw or photograph the Moon every night for a month. | KU/WS | 2 | 1 mark for indicating how the Moon's appearance will be recorded<br>1 mark for referring to the need for a number of recordings |
| **2.** 1 month | KU | 1 | Accept approximately 28–30 days |
| **3.** East<br>South<br>West | A | 1<br>1<br>1 | |
| **4a.**  | A/WS | 1 | Shadow must be directly below the stick |
| **4b.** The Sun is drawn to the left of the post. | A/WS | 1 | |
| **4c.** The Earth spins on its axis or turns. As it does so, the Sun appears to move across the sky. | KU | 2 | 1 mark for the rotation of the Earth<br>1 mark for referring to this makes it look as if the Sun is moving |

# Forces

| Test 1 (diagnostic) | Area | Mark | Extra information |
|---|---|---|---|
| **1.** True | KU | 1 | |
| **2.** False | KU | 1 | |
| **3a.** Friction | KU | 1 | |
| **3b.** The friction would be reduced. So the boxes would slide more easily or with less force. | A | 1 | Accept box and surface heat up owing to friction |
| **3c.** It will decrease. | A | 1 | |
| **4a.** Force meter or newton meter | KU/WS | 1 | Accept either |
| **4b.** Newtons or N | KU/WS | 1 | Accept either |
| **4c.** 8 N | A/WS | 1 | |
| **4d.** Box B | A/WS | 1 | |
| **5.** Less | A | 1 | |

| Test 2 (mid-topic) | Area | Mark | Extra information |
|---|---|---|---|
| **1a.** Newtons or N | KU | 1 | |
| **1b.** Gravity | KU | 1 | |
| **1c.** It slows down the parachute's fall. | KU | 1 | |
| **1d.** C: the smallest parachute | A | 1 | |
| **1e.** Reduce the parachute's load or increase its diameter. | A/WS | 1 | Accept either |
| **1f.** A stopwatch | A/WS | 1 | |
| **2a.** Water resistance | KU | 1 | Accept friction |
| **2b.** Description of a test for the different shaped boats. Description of a method for comparison between the boats or a fair test. | A/WS | 2 | 1 mark for description of test<br>1 mark for comparison or a fair test |
| **3.** To enable a rider to move the pedals (a long way) and reduce their effort to turn the rear wheel. | KU | 1 | Accept it makes it easier to pedal up a hill |

 

# Forces (continued)

| Test 3 (end of topic) | Area | Mark | Extra information |
|---|---|---|---|
| **1.** Gravity, friction, weight | KU | 1 | All circled for 1 mark |
| **2a.** An arrow, labelled air resistance, pointing back up the slide. | KU | 1 | |
| **2b.** An arrow, labelled friction, pointing back up the slide. | KU | 1 | |
| **3a.** Friction | KU | 1 | |
| **3b.** A newton meter or force meter | KU/WS | 1 | |
| **3c.** Carpet | A/WS | 1 | |
| **3d.** It is the largest force shown. | A/WS | 1 | |
| **3e.** Any **one** from:<br>Different surfaces have different friction effects.<br>Smoother surfaces have less friction.<br>Need different amounts of force to move things across different surfaces. | A/WS | 1 | |
| **4.** The two levers move across each other. Smaller force at the handles results in larger force at the cutting area. | A | 2 | 1 mark to describe how the levers move<br>1 mark to explain the action of the forces |

| Test 4 (end of year) | Area | Mark | Extra information |
|---|---|---|---|
| **1a.** Gravity | KU | 1 | |
| **1b.** Air resistance | KU | 1 | |
| **1c.** To ensure it is a fair test. | A/WS | 1 | |
| **1d.** Seconds | KU/WS | 1 | |
| **1e.** *x*-axis: width of parachute<br>*y*-axis: time | A/WS | 1 | 1 mark for both correct<br>Accept diameter of parachute |
| **1f.** The wider the parachute the slower it falls. | A/WS | 1 | |
| **1g.** The air resistance of the parachute slows the person down so they reach the ground at a lower speed. | A | 2 | 1 mark for parachute increases air resistance<br>1 mark for this results in reduced speed<br>1 mark for reduced speed increases likelihood of safe landing or decreases likelihood of damage |
| **2.** The force applied by the person is smaller and the force applied to the weight is greater. | KU | 2 | |